# How We Use

# Rock

Chris Oxlade

# www.raintreepublishers.co.uk
Visit our website to find out more information about **Raintree** books.

To order:
 ☎ Phone 44 (0) 1865 888112
▤ Send a fax to 44 (0) 1865 314091
▣ Visit the Raintree bookshop at **www.raintreepublishers.co.uk** to browse our catalogue and order online.

First published in Great Britain by Raintree,
Halley Court, Jordan Hill, Oxford OX2 8EJ,
part of Harcourt Education.
Raintree is a registered trademark of
Harcourt Education Ltd.

Editorial: Nick Hunter
Design: Kim Saar
Picture Research: Heather Sabel and Amor
   Montes de Oca
Production: Alex Lazarus

Originated by Ambassador Litho Ltd.
Printed and bound in China by South China
Printing Company

ISBN 1 844 43261 0 (hardback)
08 07 06 05 04
10 9 8 7 6 5 4 3 2 1

ISBN 1 844 43271 8 (paperback)
09 08 07 06 05
10 9 8 7 6 5 4 3 2 1

**British Library Cataloguing in Publication Data**
Oxlade, Chris
How We Use Rock. - (Using Materials)
620.1'32
A full catalogue record for this book is available from the British Library.

**Acknowledgements**
The publishers would like to thank the following for permission to reproduce photographs:
Corbis pp. **5**, **7** (Archivo Iconograifco, S. A.), **8**, **9**, **12** (ART on FILE), **13** (Wolfgang Kaehler), **15** (Darama), **21** (Reuters New Media Inc.), **24** (Michael Freeman), **25**, **27** (David Pollack), **28** (Yann Arthus-Bertrand); Heartland Images (Paul McMahon) p. **10**; Getty Images (Photodisc Green) p. **11**; Lisa Battaglene p. **23**; Photographers Direct p. **16**; Visuals Unlimited pp. **4** (Martin G. Miller), **6** (Dick Keen), **14** (Albert J. Copley), **17** (Inga Spence), **19**, **20** (Larry Stepanowicz), **22** (David Cavagniro), **26** (Larry Stepanowicz), **29** (John D. Cunningham); World Religions Photo Library (C. Osborne) p. **18**.

Cover photographs reproduced with permission of Corbis.

Every effort has been made to contact copyright holders of any material reproduced in this book. Any omissions will be rectified in subsequent printings if notice is given to the publishers.

The paper used to print this book comes from sustainable resources.

# Contents

Any words appearing in bold, **like this**, are explained in the Glossary.

# Rock and its properties

All the things we use at home, school and work are made from materials. Rock is a material. We use rocks for many different jobs. For example, builders use **slabs** of hard rock to build huge structures and jewellers use small pieces of coloured rock in delicate pieces of jewellery.

This rock is called granite. It is very hard and heavy. This close-up photograph shows the **crystals** that make up granite.

Chalk is a soft and crumbly rock. It is made of the shells of very old tiny sea creatures.

**Properties** tell us what a material is like. All rocks are **solid** except at very high temperatures. Some are hard. Some are soft. Most rocks are very heavy. Some feel rough and some feel smooth. They come in many different colours, and some have beautiful patterns and swirls.

## Don't use it!

*The different properties of materials make them useful for different jobs. These properties can also make them unsuitable for some jobs. For example, rock is* **brittle**. *That means a thin piece of rock would snap. So we do not use rock to make things that need to bend, such as fishing rods.*

# Where does rock come from?

Rock is a **natural** material. It comes from Earth's crust, which is the **solid** outer layer of the planet. If we dig into the ground anywhere we will eventually find solid rock. Most rocks we use formed hundreds of millions of years ago. Some are more than a thousand million years old.

## Getting rocks

Rocks come in many different sizes. Small rocks found on the surface of Earth are sometimes called stones or pebbles. Very large rocks might be called boulders.

Limestone rock is dug up at quarries.

These ancient tools are made from a type of rock called flint.

A place where rock is dug from the surface is called a **quarry**. Sometimes the rocks we want are buried deep underground. These rocks are much harder to get because we have to dig mines to get them out.

## The Stone Age

*A million years ago people did not have **metal** tools such as knives and axes. Nobody even knew about metals then. Instead, people made simple tools from rock by chipping them to make them sharp. They used them to hunt animals, which they cut up for food and fur. This time in history is called the Stone Age.*

# Rock for walls

Many sorts of rock are very hard. They are difficult to crush. This makes them good for building walls in houses and gardens. In a wall, the rock at the bottom of the wall supports the rock above it.

This wall is made from layers of stones on top of each other.

Walls without cement holding the rocks together are called dry-stone walls.

## Don't use it!

*Rock is very heavy. It is too heavy for building very tall structures such as skyscrapers. The heavy rock at the top of the structure would crush the rock at the bottom. So, we use **concrete** and **metal** instead.*

Rock blocks for making walls are usually cut from larger pieces of **natural** rock. The blocks are laid on top of each other and held together with a sort of glue called **cement**. Some walls are made by piling up pieces of rock found on the surface of Earth, without cutting them first.

# Rock for roads

Roads must have a tough surface so that they last a long time. Strong rock, such as granite, is perfect for this job. The rocks are crushed into small pieces and spread out to make the surface. The crushed rock is called **aggregate**. Road builders put larger stones under the road surface to stop the aggregate sinking into the ground.

Crushed rock is delivered to building sites in large trucks.

## Rocks for concrete

*Crushed rock is one of the ingredients in concrete. The rock is mixed with water and **cement**. When the mixture dries the cement goes very hard, holding the rock together. Concrete can be made into any shape by pouring it into a **mould**.*

## Smooth roads

The surface of a road is made of aggregate mixed with a black sticky material called bitumen. The bitumen holds the pieces of rock together like glue. Bitumen is **waterproof**, too. It stops water leaking into the road and washing it away.

Gravel is made up of small pieces of rock. Most gravel is made by crushing rocks against each other. We can make paths and driveways from gravel. We also use it in **concrete**.

Inside a piece of concrete you can see the tiny pieces of rock with cement around them.

# Rock surfaces

We make floors and paths from flat pieces of rock. The flat pieces are called **slabs**. Because rock is so hard, floors and paths made from rock can last for hundreds of years. Sometimes the slabs are made by cutting large pieces of rock with special saws. Sometimes they are made by hitting the rock with a hammer and chisel to make it split apart.

This path is made from chips of a rock called slate. It splits into small chips easily.

Polished marble slabs have been used to make this floor. Marble has swirls of colour in it.

## Cool rock

People like floors made from rock because it is a **natural** material and very hard wearing. In places where the weather is very hot, houses often have rock floors. A rock floor helps to keep the room cool. It also feels cool on people's feet because it **conducts** heat away from warm feet.

### Don't use it!

*We do not use stone slabs to build roads. Rock is a **brittle** material. The slabs would crack if heavy trucks rolled over them. Thousands of years ago **engineers** in ancient Rome did build roads with stone slabs. The rock did not break because only horses and small carts used these roads.*

# Using rough and smooth rock

Rocks can have different **textures**. Some rocks feel rough. Others feel smooth. Sandstone is a very rough rock. It is made from small grains of sand all stuck together. You can feel the grains when you touch the rock. Slate is a smooth rock. It is made from very tiny grains all joined together. The grains are so tiny that you cannot feel them. Slate can be used to make work surfaces and floor tiles.

The surface of sandstone feels very rough because it is made up of grains of sand.

Pumice is a sort of rough rock that comes from volcanoes. People use pumice to scrape old bits of skin off themselves!

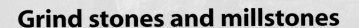

## Grind stones and millstones

Rough rocks are useful for sharpening the **metal** blades of tools. Rubbing a blade on a piece of rock called a grind stone wears away the metal to make a sharp edge. Heavy pieces of rough rock, called millstones, are used to grind corn.

### Smoothing rock

*We can cut and polish rock to make the surface very smooth. Rocks can also get polished **naturally**. For example, pebbles on the beach get polished by each other as they are rubbed together by the waves from the sea.*

# Rock for decoration

Rocks come in many different colours such as black, white and red. Some rocks have beautiful patterns in them as well. The patterns are made by the different **minerals** found in the rocks. Coloured and patterned rocks are polished to make ornaments and to decorate buildings. **Mosaics** are made from small pieces of coloured rock.

Ornaments can be made from rock. This owl is made from cut and polished marble.

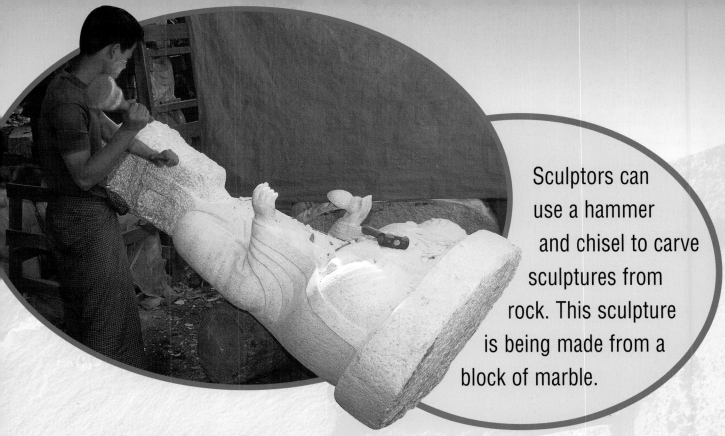

Sculptors can use a hammer and chisel to carve sculptures from rock. This sculpture is being made from a block of marble.

## Rock sculpture

Artists often use rock as a **raw material** for **sculptures**. A sculptor starts with a block of rock. He or she chips away the rock to leave a sculpture. The sculptor needs skill and practice to cut away the right bits of rock.

### Don't use it!

*Rock is a hard, **brittle** material. It cannot be bent like metal and plastic. Designers and sculptors always choose a material with the **properties** they need to make their objects and sculptures. For example, rock would not be used for a thin, delicate sculpture.*

# Heavy rocks

Rock is a heavy material. A piece of rock is usually heavier than a piece of wood or plastic of the same size. A boulder of granite the size of a car weighs many tonnes. Rocks are good for making weights. A big stone makes a good paperweight to stop papers blowing away.

This man is using a shaduf to collect water. The heavy piece of rock pulls down one side of the shaduf so that the bucket on the other side is lifted up.

Huge boulders along the shore protect it from the sea waves.

**Engineers** make use of the heaviness of rock. They put huge boulders along the seashore to stop the waves eating away at the land. Even big waves cannot move the heavy boulders, so the land behind is protected from the waves.

## Light rocks

*Some rocks are made when **lava** from a volcano cools down. Sometimes these rocks are full of air bubbles, which makes them very light. Ancient Roman engineers used light rocks to build walls. This meant they could build high walls that did not get too heavy and fall down.*

# Sand and glass

Sand is made up of millions and millions of tiny bits of rock. Each tiny bit is called a grain. Sand is made when **solid** rocks get broken down as they are bashed together by wind and water. Sand is a useful material. It is soft and it flows easily. We can use sand in sandpits for playing in and in pits for long-jumpers to land in.

If you look closely at sand you can see the tiny grains. Each one is about a millimetre across.

Bags full of sand are used to help stop floods reaching towns and cities.

Sand is also a good **abrasive**. Sand glued to a sheet of paper makes sandpaper. This rough paper is used to smooth wood and rub away old paint. Very dirty **metal** objects can be cleaned by sandblasting, which is firing a jet of sand-filled air at the object.

Sand is also a **raw material** for making glass and **concrete**. There are different kinds of glass. To make each different kind, different **chemicals** are added to the sand. Most glass is called soda glass. It is made from sand, limestone and a chemical called soda ash.

21

# Rocks and ceramics

Most rocks are hard, but some are soft. Clay is a soft material made from very tiny pieces of rock. Clay is crumbly when it is dry, and sticky when it is wet. If we put a piece of soft, wet clay in a very hot oven called a kiln it dries out and goes very hard. It stays hard even if it gets wet again. Bricks are also made from clay.

When this pot is finished it will be put in a hot oven to make it go hard.

This ceramic is called porcelain. It is made from a sort of clay called china clay.

We use clay to make vases, cups and plates. A potter makes these objects with wet clay. The shapes are put in an oven to make them go hard. This is called firing. Things made from clay are called ceramics. They do not **conduct** heat or **electricity** well. So we use them to stop electricity and heat moving. For example, overhead electricity cables are held up by ceramic supports.

## Don't use it!

*Ceramic objects are hard, but not very strong. They break easily if they are dropped or hit. So we do not make balls from ceramics.*

# Precious stones

All rocks are made of **minerals**. Most rocks are a mixture of different minerals. You can often see the different minerals because they are different colours. We use some minerals from rocks for different jobs. For example, the mineral quartz is used in electronic clocks. It makes tiny **electric** signals that keep the clock going at the right speed.

These precious stones are called rubies.

This cut diamond will be put in a piece of jewellery.

## Jewels and gemstones

Beautiful jewels and **gemstones** such as diamonds, sapphires and emeralds are minerals from rocks. Rough lumps of the minerals are carefully cut and polished to make them into shiny jewels. Jewels and gemstones are expensive because there is only a certain amount of them to be found on Earth.

### Diamonds

*Diamond is the hardest mineral of all. Large diamonds are made into jewels. Tiny diamonds (smaller than grains of sand) are used to make diamond-tipped drill bits and diamond saw blades. They can cut other very hard materials such as **metal** and rock.*

# Chemicals and minerals

We use many rocks just as they are when we find them. For example, we use **solid** rocks for building. We can also get many useful **chemicals** from the **minerals** in rocks, too. We break up the rocks to get the minerals out. Rock salt is a mineral. We use it to grit roads in the winter because it stops water from freezing as ice. We get a chemical called lime from limestone. We use lime to make **cement** and also mix it into soil to help plants grow.

In winter, trucks cover the roads with rock salt to stop cars sliding on ice and crashing.

Iron that has been melted can be poured into **moulds** to make objects. Iron comes from rock ore.

## Metals from rock

Most **metals** come from minerals in rocks. We call these rocks ores. For example, the metal iron comes from an ore called iron oxide. We find iron oxide in some types of rock. To get the iron ore we have to dig the rocks out and crush them up. The ore is heated up with other chemicals to get the iron from it.

# Rock and the environment

There is no shortage of rocks because Earth is made of rocks! We can damage Earth, though, when we dig rocks out. **Quarries** often spoil the **natural** landscape. In some places millions of trees are cut down to get at the rocks underneath them. We can sometimes **recycle** rocks instead of digging more quarries. For example, the rocks from an old house that is knocked down could be used to build something else.

Quarries make huge scars in the landscape.

These rock sculptures have been eaten away by acid rain.

## Spoiling rock

Some human activities can harm the rocks we use. **Gases** that go into the air when we burn coal in power stations can turn rain into an **acid**. This rain is known as acid rain. When acid rain falls on rocks it eats them away very slowly. Over many years buildings and outdoor **sculptures** can be ruined by acid rain.

# Find out for yourself

The best way to find out more about rocks is to investigate rocks for yourself. Look around your home and garden for things made from rock, and keep an eye out for rock through your day. Think about why rock was used for each job. What **properties** make it suitable? You will find the answers to many of your questions in this book. You can also look in other books and on the Internet.

## Books to read

*Science Answers: Grouping Materials*, Carol Ballard (Heinemann Library, 2003)

*Discovering Science: Matter*, Rebecca Hunter (Raintree, 2003)

*Science Files: Rocks and Minerals*, Steve Parker (Heinemann Library, 2002)

## Using the Internet

Try searching the Internet to find out about things to do with rock. Websites can change, so if one of the links below no longer works, don't worry. Use a search engine, such as www.yahooligans.com or www.internet4kids.com. For example, you could try searching using the keywords '**quarrying**', 'road building' and '**mineral**'.

## Websites

A great site, which explains all about different materials:
http://www.bbc.co.uk/schools/revisewise/science/materials/

A fun site that explains how rock is used:
www.qpa.org/kids.htm

# Glossary

**abrasive** rough material used to wear away another material by rubbing

**acid** liquid that can eat away at materials

**aggregate** crushed rock used to make road surfaces

**brittle** snaps easily

**cement** material used to glue together rocks in walls and concrete

**chemical** substance that we can use to make other substances

**concrete** very hard material made from rock and cement

**conduct** let heat or electricity pass through

**crystals** piece of material in which the tiny parts are rows and columns

**electricity** form of energy that flows along wires

**engineer** person who designs and makes machines and buldings

**gas** substance that flows to fill the space it is in

**gemstone** precious crystal found in rock

**lava** melted rock that flows from a volcano

**metal** hard, shiny material that conducts electricity and heat

**mineral** material that rocks are made of

**mosaic** picture or pattern made up of small pieces of material such as rock

**mould** block of metal with a space in the centre. When concrete is poured into the mould it sets, making an object the same shape as the inside of the mould.

**natural** describes anything that is not made by people

**property** quality of a material that tells us what it is like. Hard, soft, bendy and strong are all properties.

**quarry** place where rock is dug from the ground

**raw material** natural material used to make other materials

**recycle** to use material from old objects to make new objects

**sculpture** ornamental object made from materials

**slab** thick sheet of material

**solid** substance that does not flow

**texture** the way something feels

**waterproof** describes a material that does not let water pass through it

# Index